Joe Biden:
46TH US PRESIDENT

Stephen Currie

ReferencePoint
Press

San Diego, CA

About the Author

Stephen Currie is the author of several dozen books for young people, many of them for ReferencePoint Press. He has also taught at grade levels ranging from kindergarten to college. He lives with his family in New York's Hudson Valley.

For more information, contact:
ReferencePoint Press, Inc.
PO Box 27779
San Diego, CA 92198
www.ReferencePointPress.com

LIBRARY OF CONGRESS CATALOGING-IN-PUBLICATION DATA

Names: Currie, Stephen, 1960- author.
Title: Joe Biden : 46th US President / by Stephen Currie.
Description: San Diego, CA : ReferencePoint Press, 2022. | Includes
   bibliographical references and index.
Identifiers: LCCN 2021005049 (print) | LCCN 2021005050 (ebook) | ISBN
   9781678200848 (library binding) | ISBN 9781678200855 (ebook)
Subjects: LCSH: Biden, Joseph R., Jr.--Juvenile literature. |
   Presidents--United States--Juvenile literature. | Politicians--United
   States--Biography--Juvenile literature. | United States--Politics and
   government--2017---Juvenile literature. | Legislators--United
   States--Biography--Juvenile literature. | United States. Congress.
   Senate--Biography--Juvenile literature. | United States--Politics and
   government--1945-1989--Juvenile literature. | United States--Politics
   and government--1989---Juvenile literature. |
   Delaware--Biography--Juvenile literature.
Classification: LCC E917 .C87 2022 (print) | LCC E917 (ebook) | DDC
   973.934092 [B]--dc23
LC record available at https://lccn.loc.gov/2021005049
LC ebook record available at https://lccn.loc.gov/2021005050

CONTENTS

The President and the Man

On November 7, 2020, Americans in cities across the country joined together in spontaneous celebration. In Washington, DC, thousands of jubilant people congregated at Black Lives Matter Plaza near the White House. In New Orleans there was dancing in the streets. On the sidewalks of Chicago, people popped open bottles of champagne. New Yorkers cheered from their apartment windows, echoing the enthusiasm of those in the crowds below. And in business districts and residential neighborhoods from Philadelphia to Los Angeles, impromptu parties started up, drivers honked their horns, and ordinary Americans waved flags, banged on drums, and set off fireworks.

Four days had passed since Election Day, when voters throughout the country went to the polls to choose a president. The election had been close, with no clear winner on election night. As a result, major news outlets had held off calling the race for either Donald Trump, the incumbent, or Trump's challenger, Joe Biden. But as more and more votes were counted, the result became evident. On the morning of November 7, news organizations such as CNN and NBC declared that Biden had won Pennsylvania, giving him enough electoral votes to become the nation's next president. The gatherings in cities such as Washington expressed the euphoria many Biden voters felt when they heard the news. "I jumped off the bus to come right down here to the White House," said Washington resident Donna Thomas. "It is something to celebrate."[1]

The Path to the Presidency

Biden's supporters saw their candidate's victory as a triumph for their vision of America. Biden's win signaled changes in government policies ranging from climate change to transgender rights and from immigration to foreign affairs. But winning the presidency also represented a personal triumph for Biden—the pinnacle of an extraordinary career in public service. Before running in 2020, Biden had served six terms in the US Senate, followed by two four-year terms as vice president in Barack Obama's administration. The 2020 election, moreover, marked Biden's third try for the presidency. Biden has been referred to on many occasions as "the ultimate insider,"[2] a description that reflects his many years in public service.

Indeed, few political leaders in American history have had as long a career in politics and government as Biden. His career in public life began in 1970, when he won an election for county commissioner

On November 7, 2020, Joseph R. Biden addressed the nation after securing victory over Donald J. Trump.

in his home state of Delaware. Since then he has been in elective office almost continuously—and during much of the time he spent out of office, he was running a presidential campaign. Given his years of service, Biden's career has had a number of distinctions. His election to the US Senate weeks before his thirtieth birthday made him one of the youngest senators ever to serve. His thirty-six years in the Senate place him among the longest-serving senators in American history. And by taking the oath of office at age seventy-eight, Biden became the oldest person ever to serve as US president.

For Biden, though, the road to the presidency was far from easy. As a boy he experienced occasional economic insecurity. Though his family could usually afford the basics of food, clothing, and shelter, there were not a lot of extras. Biden also had a significant stutter, which made him a frequent target of teasing. As an adult, he survived a major medical condition that threatened his life. In addition, Biden experienced two family tragedies. The first, a car crash in 1972, killed his first wife and their daughter while seriously injuring their two sons. The second was the death of one of those sons to a rare form of brain cancer in 2015. Biden "is the unluckiest person I've ever known personally,"[3] says his friend Ted Kaufman, who succeeded him in the Senate.

Nonetheless, Biden persevered. Despite obstacles, disappointments, and tragedy, Biden never gave up. Instead, he continued to move forward, whether that meant working to overcome his stutter, changing his lifestyle in order to support his family, or running for office in an effort to make America the best country it could be. As he once put it, "Failure at some point in your life is inevitable, but giving up is unforgivable."[4] In this way Biden has led not just by his words and votes as a political figure but by his own example as a human being. This combination of the personal and the political has marked Biden's life and work since the beginning.

"Failure at some point in your life is inevitable, but giving up is unforgivable."[4]

—Joe Biden

CHAPTER ONE

Early Years

The presidents of the United States have come from all walks of life, but many of them share a few characteristics. Several presidents, for example, came from highly political families. George W. Bush and John Quincy Adams were the sons of presidents, and Benjamin Harrison was the grandson of one. Being born into a wealthy family is also a common trait of many presidents. Donald Trump's father was a billionaire who made most of his money in the New York City real estate market. John Kennedy's father built a large family fortune as an investor and entrepreneur. Franklin Roosevelt was born into one of New York's oldest and wealthiest families.

In addition, many presidents have distinguished themselves as soldiers or scholars. George Washington, of course, was a general in the Revolutionary War. Ulysses S. Grant, Dwight Eisenhower, and Andrew Jackson likewise served as military commanders and were then elected to the presidency. As for academics, many presidents have attended highly selective and prestigious schools. Eight, including Barack Obama, Teddy Roosevelt, and Franklin Roosevelt, obtained degrees from Harvard University, and five graduated from Yale University. Others, including Thomas Jefferson and Woodrow Wilson, were known for their intellect—Wilson remains the only president to have earned a doctorate.

Though most presidents fit into at least one of these categories, Joe Biden, the forty-sixth president, does not. None of Biden's parents or grandparents held elective office or were especially involved in politics. Neither did Biden come from wealth. His father worked a sequence of sales and blue-collar jobs, and the family was often short of money. Biden has written about times when he was forced to "put cardboard in an old shoe till Dad's next payday"[5] instead of buying a new pair. Biden never served in the armed forces, let alone in a position of military leadership, and he was by his own admission an indifferent student whose academic career was undistinguished. He had little in common, then, with Kennedy, the Bushes, the Roosevelts, or indeed most other presidents of the past, and there were few indications that someday his name would be known across the world.

Yet Biden's experiences in his early years did serve as an excellent foundation for a career in government. Perhaps most critically, he learned the importance of determination—a value exemplified and encouraged by both his parents. "The world dropped you on your head?" Biden remembered years later. "My dad would say, *Get up!* You're lying in bed feeling sorry for yourself? *Get up!*"[6] As a young man, Biden also showed flashes of leadership, especially in sports. He struck many people as kind, compassionate, and honest. And even though he did not always apply himself academically, Biden often impressed friends and teachers with his intelligence. Biden did not grow up in a well-off political family, nor did he make his mark as a commander or a scholar. But his early years nonetheless helped prepare him for one of the most difficult jobs on earth.

Scranton to Wilmington

Joseph Robinette Biden Jr. was born on November 20, 1942, in the industrial city of Scranton in northeastern Pennsylvania. He was the oldest of four children born to Joe Sr. and Jean Finnegan Biden; the other three were Valerie, Jimmy, and Frankie. For the first decade of his life, Joe Jr. lived mainly in Scranton, a period that he remembers with great fondness. His mother was a Scranton native, and young Joe spent much of his time with her extended family. When Joe was ten, the family left Scranton to move about 140 miles (225 km) south to the outskirts of Wilmington, Delaware, where jobs were said to be more plentiful. Indeed, Joe's father soon found work managing a car dealership. For many years the Bidens returned to Scranton whenever they could to spend weekends with their Finnegan relatives.

But Joe's nuclear family was even more important in his growth and development. He was very close to his sister and brothers. While they still lived in Scranton, Joe would put Valerie on the handlebars of his bicycle to give her a ride to a nearby playground. If one sibling was threatened or teased by neighborhood children, the other siblings typically came to his or her defense. Joe also admired both his parents, whom he credits with instilling a strong sense of right and wrong in their children. He also saw them as kind and loving people who wanted their children to succeed. That included giving them pep talks when the children were discouraged. "Remember, Joey, you're a Biden," he recalls his mother telling him. "Nobody is better than you. You're not better than anybody else, but *nobody* is better than you."[7]

The lessons Joe learned at home were reinforced at school and at church. The Bidens were Roman Catholic, and as a boy Joe attended services regularly. He was enrolled in parochial school, first in Pennsylvania and then in Delaware. His instructors "taught reading and writing and math and geography and history," Biden remembers, "but embedded in the curriculum also were the concepts of decency, fair play, and virtue."[8] Upon completing eighth grade, Joe hoped to attend Archmere Academy, a Catholic high school. The tuition was more than his parents could afford, but the school offered Joe the chance to work around the campus during the summer and apply his earnings toward the cost of the program. He entered Archmere in the fall of 1957.

> "Remember, Joey, you're a Biden. Nobody is better than you. You're not better than anybody else, but *nobody* is better than you."[7]
>
> —Jean Finnegan Biden, mother to Joe Biden

Initially, Joe had difficulty at Archmere. The main reason was a speech impediment: Joe had stuttered since early childhood. In fact, due to the stutter, Archmere released him during his freshman year from the standard requirement of giving a speech to the assembled students. Joe had always been teased about the stutter, but his Archmere classmates mocked him mercilessly. Among other names, they called him "Joe Impedimenta."[9] The teasing pushed Joe to overcome the problem. He memorized passages from literature and practiced saying them fluently in front of a mirror. "If I saw my jaw start to clench," he remembered years later, "I'd pause, try to go slack, smile, then pick it up again."[10] Over time Joe's stutter became less noticeable. As a sophomore, he delivered an assigned speech without a hitch.

Joe was not a strong student at Archmere; by his own admission, he was mostly a B-average student. He did enjoy himself, though, making plenty of friends and becoming one of Arch-

Though Joe Biden has been a Delaware resident for most of his life, his presidential campaigns have also stressed his connection to Scranton, Pennsylvania, the city of his birth. On Election Day 2020, for example, he visited Scranton to remind local voters that he was one of them. "He's from Scranton, North Washington Avenue," said Janet Evans, a retired teacher, "and we the people love him and trust him." The trek to Scranton did not hurt; Biden won Scranton's Lackawanna County by almost ten thousand votes, helping him capture Pennsylvania.

The city has fallen on hard times, though, since Biden was a boy. In the early 1900s Lackawanna County was a center of the coal mining industry, a railroad hub, and a manufacturing area known for producing phonograph records. By 1942, when Biden was born, the city's population exceeded 140,000. But after 1945 Americans increasingly relied on oil and natural gas to heat their homes rather than coal, leading to economic stress in Scranton as the mines closed one by one. At the same time manufacturers shut down or moved elsewhere, and rail traffic diminished as well. Today Scranton's population is only 75,000.

Quoted in Nina Lakhani, "Joe Biden Returns to Childhood Home in Scranton: From This House to the White House," *The Guardian* (Manchester, UK), November 3, 2020. www.theguardian.com.

mere's most popular students. "He was an outgoing person, very sociable," one friend remembers, adding that Joe was the kind of person who "would talk with anybody."[11] Joe served as class president both his junior and senior years. He was also a talented football player, leading the team in scoring during his senior season. His coach once described him as "one of the best pass receivers I had in 16 years as a coach."[12] In 1961 Joe Biden graduated from Archmere and went off to the University of Delaware in nearby Newark.

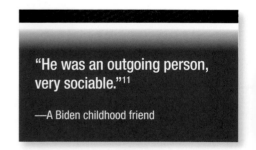

"He was an outgoing person, very sociable."[11]

—A Biden childhood friend

College

Biden had not distinguished himself academically in high school, and at first his college work was equally unimpressive. Rather than putting his energies into studying, he focused much more on dating, friends, and sports. "I probably started my first year of college a little too interested in football and meeting new girls," Biden admitted later, adding drily that "there were a lot of new girls to meet."[13] Biden's first-semester grades were poor enough that his parents told him he had to quit the freshman football team until he showed significant academic improvement. Embarrassed, Biden worked a little harder during the next few semesters, but his grades did not improve by much.

Although Biden remained a mediocre student, his friends recognized his intellectual capacity. "Joe was the kind of guy who could read someone else's notes and do better on the exam than the guy who made the notes,"[14] remembers his roommate, Donald Brunner. That innate academic ability served Biden well around the middle of his college years, when he decided that he wanted to go to law school after his graduation from the University of Delaware. Law schools are selective and use applicants' grades as an important part of admissions decisions. It was clear to Biden that his grades to that point would not qualify him for most law schools. He consequently began studying as hard as possible. In

Biden stands at the podium with his sister, Valerie Biden Owens, in 2010. As a child, Joe was close to his sister and his brothers.

the end he raised his grade point average considerably and was accepted by the law school at Syracuse University in New York.

Syracuse was not a top-ranked law school, but Biden's choice to go there was based not on reputation but on love. During a college spring break, he had met a Syracuse student named Neilia Hunter. The couple quickly began a long-distance relationship. Biden frequently made the trip to Syracuse during his final semesters of college to visit his girlfriend, and he chose to attend law school there largely to be closer to her. There were a few difficulties at first. Biden was somewhat intimidated by Hunter's family, which was much wealthier than his own. Moreover, the Hunters were Protestant, and Neilia's father was initially reluctant to allow his daughter to date a Roman Catholic. Nonetheless, these issues were eventually resolved. Joe and Neilia married in 1966, following Biden's first year of law school.

> "Joe was the kind of guy who could read someone else's notes and do better on the exam than the guy who made the notes."[14]
>
> —Donald Brunner, Joe Biden's college roommate

Law School and Beyond

Biden had not been a rousing academic success in either high school or college, and the same pattern held for law school. He frequently cut classes and failed to study as hard as he needed to. The work did not appeal to him—law school was "the biggest bore in the world,"[15] he said once—and his grades showed his overall lack of engagement. Typically, Biden did little work until near the end of the semester, when he pushed himself to learn all the material in just a few days—often with Neilia's help. It was not the most successful of strategies. At one point Biden improperly cited sources in an assignment, was accused of plagiarism, and was required to repeat the course. He did graduate in 1968, but his grades ranked him just seventy-sixth in a class of eighty-five. It was not a distinguished beginning to a legal career.

Joe and Neilia returned to Delaware in 1968. In 1969 their son Joseph III was born; they called him Beau. The following year saw the arrival of Beau's brother, Hunter. Joe and Neilia kept themselves busy with the children. They also had part-time work managing a swimming pool at a country club, along with owning a few rental properties. Biden's law degree initially got him a job working for a corporate law firm, but he soon decided that this was not the kind of work he wanted to do. The firm primarily represented wealthy and powerful clients in business and industry, and Biden realized that his heart was on the side of poorer people who had fewer resources and desperately needed the help of a skilled lawyer.

Biden stands next to his first wife, Neilia, with their two young sons, Beau and Hunter, in the summer of 1972.

In the summer of 1962, Biden got a job as a lifeguard at Prices Run, a public pool in Wilmington. At the time, Wilmington was heavily segregated. Because Prices Run was in a largely Black neighborhood, the vast majority of the people who used the pool were African American. So were all the lifeguards except Biden, who at the time was a nineteen-year-old college student. Biden's summer at Prices Run opened his eyes to the segregated nature of his city—and the discrimination and frustrations his fellow lifeguards faced. As he wrote, "Most of all I remember the stories they'd tell about how they were treated by whites day in and day out. Every day, it seemed to me, black people got subtle and not-so-subtle reminders that they didn't belong in America. It was a dozen small cuts a day. The stories my friends at the pool told were always tinged more with confusion and pain than outright anger." To this day, Biden credits his summer as a lifeguard for his later advocacy of civil rights.

Joe Biden, *Promises to Keep.* New York: Random House, 2007, p. 44.

Leaving the law firm, Biden went to work for the public defender's office. In this role he argued on behalf of accused criminals, a job he found better suited to his ideals. Unfortunately, the work was not full time, and it paid poorly. To earn extra money Biden also did some work in another lawyer's office, focusing on civil cases—that is, cases in which one party sues another with no allegation of criminal activity. But Biden soon moved on from those jobs as well. Instead, he and another attorney decided to form their own law firm, Biden and Walsh.

Through 1969, then, nothing about Biden's life indicated that he would someday be one of the most famous people on earth. Biden had not distinguished himself as a student, and he did not know the sorts of important and influential people who could push his career forward. His intelligence, his leadership skills, and his ability to get along with others were unquestioned, but he did not appear to be moving in a direction that would lead to becoming a national leader. But in 1970 Biden rather unexpectedly found a new arena in which to put his energies—an arena that would change his life considerably and eventually make him a household name.

CHAPTER TWO

Politics and Tragedy

Today Delaware is a heavily Democratic state. As of 2021 the state legislature consisted of forty Democrats and twenty-two Republicans. Delaware has not elected a Republican governor since 1988 and has voted for the Democrat in every presidential election since then as well. But the Democrats did not always dominate Delaware politics. In the early 1970s, in fact, the Republicans reigned supreme. The state legislature had more than twice as many Republicans as Democrats. The governor was a Republican, as was the state's attorney general. The state's US representative was a Republican as well. And both US senators were Republicans. In moving back to Delaware, Biden was returning to a place where the Democratic Party was largely an afterthought.

As a student, Biden had taken an interest in politics. But when he finished law school, he was not entirely sure which political party he preferred. Most of his Finnegan relatives had leaned toward the Democrats, and Biden had been inspired by the 1960 election of President John Kennedy. Kennedy was a Democrat and, like Biden, a Roman Catholic. On the other hand, some of the most influential Democrats in Delaware were defenders of racial segregation, a practice that Biden found appalling. Biden also admired some of Delaware's Republican leaders. For a time Biden called himself a political independent. Indeed, he was briefly drawn to the Republican Party. "I thought of myself as a Republican for six or seven months,"[16] he recalled years later.

But Biden's fling with Republicanism did not last. In 1969 he joined the Democrats, prompted in large part by his intense dislike of Richard Nixon, a Republican who had been elected president the previous year. Local party

leaders took notice of Biden. A lawyer Biden knew invited him to join a committee tasked with finding ways to revitalize the state's Democratic Party. Between his law practice, his growing family, and his property management, Biden had little spare time. Still, he was intrigued by the offer and decided to join. Biden evidently made a strong impression on his fellow committee members, since they asked him to consider running for the New Castle County Council—in effect the legislature of Delaware's most populous county.

Biden was unsure at first. "I had no great interest in being a county councilman,"[17] he wrote in an autobiography. However, he and Neilia eventually agreed that he should run. Biden did not expect to win the race—the district where he lived had more Republican voters than Democrats—but he concluded that running for a council seat would be a good experience if he ever decided to run for some other office in the future. Biden also knew that running a campaign, even for this relatively low-level office, would widen his circle of political and business contacts. He enlisted his sister, Valerie, to be his campaign manager and spent weeks talking to voters—especially middle-class voters, with whom he felt a particular connection. On Election Day 1970, to Biden's surprise, he won by about two thousand votes.

Eye on the Senate

As a council member, Biden made a name for himself by advocating for smart growth—that is, restricting development in order to cut down on pollution and urban sprawl. Several large factories and other companies had recently moved into the county, and while these businesses provided jobs for the people of the region, they often damaged the environment. The new businesses

Today political campaigns are thoroughly data driven. Staffers and volunteers make use of computer-generated lists of voters and keep close tabs on how individuals are likely to vote—and how likely they are to go to the polls. In the early 1970s, though, this sort of deep organization was missing from most campaigns. Biden's first political races were an exception, however. As he wrote years later:

> Val had run a very modern campaign for my council race in 1970. We got the motor vehicle registration and voter records and organized block by block. We had every development, every street in it, and every house on it on file cards. We had recruited block captains and put them to work. And for the Senate race we just built on that; Delaware wasn't that big—only one congressional district. We just used volunteers and made the file cards statewide.

Joe Biden, *Promises to Keep.* New York: Random House, 2007, p. 66.

paved over meadows, dumped waste into waterways, and added to already overloaded sewage systems. Biden was particularly concerned about plans to build an oil refinery on the Delaware River, which he feared would pollute both the air and the water. "I became known as the guy who took on the builders and the big corporations,"[18] Biden remembers. Some of the other council members charged that Biden was impeding progress, but others offered their support.

Biden's profile as a council member was high enough that he was soon asked to join the Democratic Renewal Commission, another organization trying to promote Democratic candidates in Delaware. By now Biden was busier than ever, with two council meetings each week, along with the work involved in his law practice. Moreover, he and Neilia became parents for the third time in 1971 with the birth of their daughter Naomi, nicknamed Amy. But Biden and his wife decided once again that joining the commission made sense. As with running for the county council, being part of the commission would bring him into contact with influential Democrats and perhaps lead to something bigger in the future.

The Democratic Renewal Commission had several responsibilities. Chief among them was to find a candidate to oppose incumbent Republican senator J. Caleb Boggs in the election of 1972. This was not an easy task. A World War II veteran, Boggs had already spent twelve years in the Senate and had been a two-term governor before that. He had a powerful network of friends and allies, and he was popular throughout the state. Biden and other commission members tried to recruit several Democratic politicians and corporate leaders to run for the seat, but they all declined to take on Boggs. In desperation, Democratic leaders turned to the commission's youngest member: Joe Biden. During the summer of 1971, they asked him to be their candidate.

At first Biden was startled, even shocked. He recognized that he was very young to run for such an important office. Indeed, the US Constitution mandates that senators be at least thirty years old, and Biden's thirtieth birthday would arrive just weeks before the next Senate session began. He also knew that he was inexperienced and unknown, particularly in comparison to Boggs. But the idea of being a senator deeply appealed to him. "I couldn't stop thinking about it," Biden wrote years later. "As a senator I knew I could have an effect on the issues that mattered to me: war and peace, the environment, crime, civil rights, women's rights."[19] Once again, he turned to his wife for guidance. Recognizing her husband's drive and ambition to succeed in politics, Neilia encouraged him to run. Later in 1971, Biden officially announced that he would be running for Boggs's Senate seat.

The Senate Campaign

To say that Biden was an underdog in the campaign would be a massive understatement. His candidacy seemed doomed from the start. Polls taken in the summer of 1972 suggested that the election would be a rout. At one point the well-known and popular Boggs had the support of 47 percent of Delaware voters, while just 19 percent backed Biden. It was difficult to see how Biden could win the race. Some of his allies worried that an overwhelming loss would damage any future political ambitions Biden might have. "Even the Republicans scratched their heads over why such an inexperienced—albeit attractive—candidate would seek to end his political career so abruptly,"[20] writes William B. Golin, who worked in Biden's county council campaign as a high school student.

But Biden was willing to try. As he had in his run for county council, he enlisted family members to help. Valerie served again as her brother's campaign manager. "I was the campaign manager because I was the only one who took him seriously,"[21] she remembered years later. Biden's mother organized campaign coffees, get-togethers where Biden could meet voters in the homes of supporters. Biden's brother Jimmy was put in charge of fundraising; his brother Frankie coordinated volunteers. Indeed, Biden relied on an army of enthusiastic campaign workers willing to donate their time, many of them people his age and younger. Biden did get support from an important labor union, the AFL-CIO. But for the most part he got little help from outside organizations. Even the Democratic Senatorial Campaign Committee, charged with providing assistance to Democrats running for the Senate, refused Biden funding at first; committee members preferred to put resources into more winnable races instead.

> "I was the campaign manager because I was the only one who took him seriously."[21]
>
> —Joe Biden's sister Valerie

Little by little, though, Biden made progress. When voters took the time to listen to his speeches or read his campaign materials, they often found that they agreed with his policies. One of the main campaign issues for Biden was the Vietnam War, which by 1972 was going badly for the United States. Biden strongly supported withdrawing troops and ending the war as soon as possible, a position that appealed especially to younger voters. He also championed civil rights legislation, environmental awareness, and a more equitable tax system. In addition, Biden embraced his status as a political newcomer. "Politicians have done such a job on the people that

During Biden's US Senate campaign in 1972, one of the main issues was the Vietnam War, which he strongly opposed.

the people don't believe them anymore," he argued in a radio ad, "and I'd like a shot at changing that."[22]

Voters also found Biden personally appealing. An excellent speaker, Biden was comfortable giving speeches to large groups, but he was even better at one-on-one conversation. Many voters found him enthusiastic, intelligent, and kind. "He was the Energizer Bunny," remembers one volunteer. "He'd never stop. If you went to a high school football game on a Saturday morning, he was there. . . . He'd shake hands. He had that smile, that grin."[23] Biden's wife and children proved to be an asset as well. On the campaign trail, Biden made it clear that he was not just a politician but a husband and father as well—another way in which he was able to connect with ordinary voters, especially those with young families of their own.

> "He'd never stop. If you went to a high school football game on a Saturday morning, he was there. . . . He'd shake hands. He had that smile, that grin."[23]
>
> —A volunteer in Biden's first Senate campaign

Some holidays are celebrated across the United States, but others are specific to individual states. One of the most unusual is Return Day, which is observed in Delaware on the Thursday following each Election Day. Though canceled in 2020 because of COVID-19, it has been celebrated in the state for over a century—and some experts say its roots date to before 1800.

The function of Return Day is to honor the candidates for each political office and to serve as a reminder that in a democracy, government control often moves from one political party to another. Winning and losing candidates ride together in a carriage in the community of Georgetown. Later, a hatchet is buried to symbolize the peaceful transition of power. The mood is festive, with food, music, and parades.

When Joe Biden won the 1972 Senate race, however, he was not certain he wanted to take part in this tradition. Given his unlikely victory, Biden expected that losing candidate J. Caleb Boggs would be embarrassed to ride in the carriage with him. Biden offered to skip the ceremony. But Boggs refused. "I'd be proud to ride with you," he told Biden, and the tradition continued.

Quoted in Joe Biden, *Promises to Keep*. New York: Random House, 2007, p. 74.

At first, Boggs largely ignored his young challenger. But as Election Day approached and Boggs saw his lead dwindling, the senator fought back. Hoping to convince voters that Biden's proposals were unrealistic and too expensive, he ran an ad showing a picture of the moon with the caption "The Only Thing Joe Biden Hasn't Promised You."[24] Voters, however, were not swayed. Though Republican presidential candidate Richard Nixon carried Delaware by twenty percentage points in the November 1972 election, Boggs could not hold on to his lead. In a major upset, Biden won with 50.5 percent of the votes, a margin of just over three thousand ballots. Against the odds, he had become a US senator—one of the very youngest in history.

Heartbreak

Biden immediately began preparing for his Senate career. He needed to hire staff, find a place to live in Washington, and acquaint himself with other senators. It was a busy but exciting time for Biden and his young family. "The doors were just beginning to swing open on the rest of our lives," Biden remembered years later. "Neilia and I had done this amazing thing together, and there was so much more we could do."[25] On the morning of December 18, Biden left Delaware for Washington to interview prospective staff members. Biden's wife and children stayed behind; Neilia planned to do some holiday shopping, including buying a Christmas tree.

Later that day, however, family members broke the news to Biden that Neilia's car had collided with a truck. Neilia and Naomi had been killed instantly, and Beau and Hunter were in serious condition at a local hospital. "I could not speak," Biden says of

On January 5, 1973, Biden is sworn in as US senator, accompanied by his father-in-law, Robert Hunter, holding the Bible. He was sworn in at the hospital where his sons were still being treated after a car accident in which Biden's first wife and daughter were killed.

his reaction to learning what had happened, "only felt this hollow core grow in my chest, like I was going to be sucked inside a black hole."[26] In the days that followed, Biden seldom left his sons' hospital room. Devastated over the loss of his wife and daughter and the injuries to his sons, he briefly considered ending his own life. Only the thought of what his suicide would do to Beau and Hunter kept him going.

Under the circumstances, Biden could not imagine taking his seat in the Senate. A few days after the accident, he told Senate Majority Leader Mike Mansfield of Montana that he would not serve. Delaware, Biden pointed out, could easily replace him with another senator, but his sons could not replace him with a different father. Mansfield, however, reminded Biden that Neilia had been overjoyed to see him win the election and argued that she would have wanted Biden to serve. He also told Biden that joining the Senate did not need to be permanent. "Just give me six months," he said. "If you don't feel that you're up for it, you can quit."[27]

In the end, Biden agreed to take his seat. In the wake of the tragedy, though, he made an important change in plans. The boys were in no shape to move to Washington, and Biden decided it would be best to stay close to family members. Instead of finding a place to stay in the District of Columbia, he would continue to live in his house in Delaware—and commute every day to the US Capitol, a two-hour journey by train. On January 5, 1973, Biden took his oath of office in his sons' hospital room. A year earlier he had been a little-known county commissioner. Now he was a member of the US Senate. Biden's impressive rise was overshadowed by the tragedy of the previous month. Nonetheless, he obeyed his father's words; he got up and kept going.

CHAPTER THREE

Senator Biden

Biden entered the Senate expecting that he might only stay for six months. Instead, he stayed for six terms. Not surprisingly, given the length of time he was in office, Biden's years as a member of the Senate were eventful. Over time, he became a respected leader who captured more than his share of headlines. He also became involved in several significant controversies and ran for president as well. Between 1973, when Biden joined the Senate, and 2009, when he left it, Biden had become one of America's most influential politicians.

Beginnings

Biden's Senate career got off to a rocky start. Because of his daily commute, Biden had few opportunities to get to know his colleagues. While other senators were dining together, Biden was traveling home to his sons in Wilmington. (His sister and her husband moved in with him to help take care of Hunter and Beau.) Biden also felt intimidated by his older colleagues. The biggest issue, though, was lack of motivation. Biden found it difficult at first to think of anything other than the accident that had taken the lives of his wife and daughter. "I did what was necessary and no more," he remembered later. "Losing Neilia and Naomi had taken all the joy out of being a United States senator."[28]

As time went on, however, Biden warmed to his new job. Several colleagues took the time to introduce Biden to other senators and explain the workings of the Senate to him. Biden was drawn mostly to other Democrats, but he also got to know and even appreciate some Republicans. Notable among these was South Carolina's Strom Thurmond, a staunch opponent of civil rights legislation. Biden, who supported civil rights, expected to dislike Thurmond. "But then I met the man," he wrote. "I tried to understand him. I learned from him. And I watched him change."[29] The two became friends.

Biden also realized that he enjoyed the work of making and passing laws. He began a push for campaign finance reform that would have the federal government underwriting the cost of political campaigns instead of requiring candidates to raise their own funds. Public financing, Biden contended, would reduce the impact of corporate money in politics. However, the proposal was unpopular among Biden's Senate colleagues, most of whom were effective fund-raisers who had no desire to help potential challengers. "Keep making speeches like you made today," James Eastland of Mississippi told Biden after the young senator raised the issue, "and you gonna be the youngest one-term senator in the history of America."[30]

> "Keep making speeches like you made today and you gonna be the youngest one-term senator in the history of America."[30]
>
> —James Eastland, senator from Mississippi

Biden on the Issues

Biden took Eastland's advice and stopped talking about campaign finance reform. Instead, he pushed for legislation protecting the environment, securing civil rights, and making health care more available to the middle class and the poor. At the end of the six months he had promised Mike Mansfield, Biden realized that he had no desire to leave the Senate. Indeed, he ran for reelection in 1978, this time winning 58 percent of the vote. He won again in 1984, 1990, 1996, 2002, and 2008, generally coasting to victory by about twenty percentage points. After his first election, he was never seriously challenged again.

In the US Senate, Biden became friends with Republican Strom Thurmond, despite the South Carolina senator's opposition to civil rights.

Over time, Biden became interested in other issues as well. In particular, he became known for his involvement in foreign policy. In 1979, for example, he helped negotiate an arms control treaty with the Soviet Union, an enemy of the United States at the time. Later, in 1986, Biden took on South Africa and its system of apartheid, a discriminatory system that denied rights to the country's black majority. When the president at the time, Ronald Reagan, supported South Africa despite its racist laws, Biden erupted during a Senate committee meeting. "I'm ashamed of the lack of moral backbone to this policy,"[31] he told an administration official.

Biden worked hard on matters of social justice within America, too. During the 1980s, for example, Biden grew concerned about domestic abuse and sexual assault. He noted that abusers were rarely brought to justice; moreover, he pointed out that the legal system all too often seemed to blame women for being beaten or raped. In 1990 he sponsored a piece of legislation that would

During a Senate hearing in 1986, Biden denounced America's support of South Africa, which at the time practiced strict racial segregation, a system known as apartheid.

strengthen penalties for the abuse of women. Four years later it passed both the Senate and the House and became known as the Violence Against Women Act. Years later Biden described the bill as his "proudest legislative achievement."[32]

Liberal or Conservative?

As a senator, Biden took liberal positions on most issues. He believed that government should improve people's lives, and he was willing to spend public money toward that goal. Biden was an enthusiastic supporter of Social Security and other government programs designed to help retirees and the needy, and he routinely argued against attempts to cut benefits. "The best measure of the humaneness of a society," he once declared, "is the way in which a society treats its elderly."[33] Biden also advocated spending for mass transit. As a daily user of Amtrak, the passenger train system heavily supported by the federal government, he opposed measures designed to limit its funding.

However, Biden was noted for his willingness to work with his political opponents. "It's not always enough to bring along my political allies," he writes. "Sometimes I need the support of people who fundamentally disagree with me on 80 percent of the questions we decide."[34] He set out to convince others through facts and logic, of course; but he also relied on personal connections such as the one he had formed with Thurmond. Biden cultivated a reputation as a man who could be trusted and who treated others with respect. His work paid off. Through his time in the Senate, he frequently convinced Republicans as well as Democrats to join him in supporting legislation.

And on some issues, Biden departed from liberal orthodoxy. One example was the busing controversy of the early 1970s. Busing was a plan to desegregate schools by sending White children to heavily Black schools and vice versa. Because busing was a civil rights issue, many liberals supported it. Biden, however, did

> "The best measure of the humaneness of a society is the way in which a society treats its elderly."[33]
>
> —Joe Biden

Medical Trauma

In February 1988 Biden unexpectedly developed an aneurysm, or a bulging blood vessel in his brain. By the time the condition was discovered, some of Biden's blood had already leaked out into the surrounding brain tissue. Doctors told him that if any more blood escaped, he would likely die. Biden needed emergency surgery, which required transferring him by ambulance from a Wilmington hospital to Walter Reed Army Medical Center outside Washington, DC. He was given only a 50 percent chance of surviving the surgery—and if he did survive, the odds were good that his brain function would be diminished.

Biden was fortunate; the surgery was successful. While the recovery period was long, he suffered no lasting damage from the operation. But Biden's ordeal was not yet over. First, doctors put him back in the hospital when they discovered a blood clot, a sort of plug in the blood vessels, which they feared might get into his lungs and kill him. When the danger from the clot was past, surgeons performed another operation to repair a second aneurysm. In all, Biden missed more than six months of work in the Senate.

not. Mandatory busing, he said, violated "the cardinal rule of common sense."[35] Later, in 2005, Biden was one of the few Democrats in Congress to support legislation that favored credit card companies over consumers. On both issues, Biden was influenced by his constituents. Most Delaware residents opposed busing in the 1970s, and Delaware is home to many finance corporations.

Controversies

Anyone serving six terms in Congress is likely to generate some controversy, and Biden was no exception. In 1987 President Reagan nominated legal scholar and judge Robert Bork to fill a vacancy on the Supreme Court. All federal judges, including Supreme Court justices, must be confirmed by the Senate in order to serve. Bork's credentials were impressive, and his confirmation seemed assured. To that point in US history, nominees of Bork's caliber had seldom been rejected. But Biden, then the chair of the Senate Judiciary Committee, worried about Bork's extreme conservatism. He subjected the nominee to difficult questions in Senate hearings and encouraged others to vote against confirmation. Bork's nomination was rejected. Conservatives complained bitterly, but in vain, that Biden was wrong to base his vote on politics rather than on competence.

Four years later, President George H.W. Bush nominated a federal judge named Clarence Thomas to serve on the Supreme Court. Before the Senate voted, though, a law professor named Anita Hill testified before the Senate Judiciary Committee that Thomas had sexually harassed her. When asked to respond, Thomas denied the allegations. Liberals believed Hill. Conservatives believed Thomas. In the end, Thomas was narrowly confirmed. Biden voted against the nomination, but that did not spare him from criticism. At least three other women notified the committee that they, like Hill, had been sexually harassed by Thomas. As a leader on the committee, Biden could have called these women to testify. But he did not. Quite a few people on the left have not forgiven Biden for his inaction. "He did everything to

There are many stories about Joe Biden's integrity and kindness. One of the most compelling is told by a rabbi named Michael Beals. During the early 2000s a Delaware woman named Sheila Greenhouse passed away, and Beals went to her apartment building to conduct a worship service in celebration of her life. Because Greenhouse's apartment was small, Beals led the service in the building's communal laundry room. At one point, Beals wrote years later, he looked up and was shocked to see Biden enter the room. After the service, Beals asked Biden why he was present.

"Listen," Biden told Beals, "back in 1972, when I first ran for Senate, Mrs. Greenhouse gave $18 to my first campaign. Because that's what she could afford. And every six years, when I'd run for reelection, she'd give another $18. She did it her whole life. I'm here to show my respect and gratitude."

Beals went on to explain that the number *18* is of special significance in his faith. "But it's also a humble amount," he wrote. "Joe Biden knew that. And he respected that. . . . Joe Biden didn't come to that service for political gain. He came to that service because he has character."

Michael Beals, "I Know Joe Biden: Rabbi Michael Beals." Medium, September 9, 2019. https://medium.com.

make [the hearings] be good for Thomas," said one of Hill's lawyers years later, "and slant it against [Hill]."[36]

Biden took other controversial positions as well. In 2002 President George W. Bush pushed for the United States to invade Iraq. In order to declare war, Bush needed congressional approval. As the chair of the Senate Foreign Relations Committee, Biden could call witnesses who would argue for or against an invasion. Most Democrats opposed the war and expected that Biden would call witnesses who were on their side. Instead, most of the witnesses Biden called agreed with Bush, and Biden ultimately voted for a declaration of war. Though Biden quickly came to regret his vote, some observers remain angry. "Biden should explain why he played such a major role"[37] in authorizing the war, wrote commentator Mark Weisbrot in 2020.

A Presidential Run

While Biden enjoyed being a senator, he soon developed bigger ambitions: to be president. As the election of 1988 approached,

Biden decided that the timing was right. He was finishing a third term in the Senate, so lack of experience was not an issue, and with Reagan retiring there would be no incumbent in the race. In June 1987 Biden officially entered the presidential race, announcing his candidacy in a speech that stressed the need for Americans to work together. "For too long in this society, we have celebrated unrestrained individualism over common community," Biden charged. "We must rekindle the fire of idealism in our society, for nothing suffocates the promise of America more than unbounded cynicism and indifference."[38] By late summer, Biden was considered one of the top Democratic candidates.

Then disaster struck. In August Biden gave a speech in which he contrasted his own educational background with those of his parents and grandparents. "I started thinking as I was coming over here, why is it that Joe Biden is the first in his family ever to go to a university?" he asked his audience. "Is it because I'm the first Biden in a thousand generations to get a college and a graduate degree that I was smarter than the rest?"[39] Biden went on to discuss his coal miner ancestors and their interest in poetry. It was an effective speech with an important message about hard work and upward mobility. But it was not Biden's own creation. Earlier that year British politician Neil Kinnock had given a speech about his own life in which he made exactly the same points in almost the same language.

Another candidate's campaign quickly alerted the media to the similarities between the speeches. Biden was accused not only of plagiarism but of commandeering Kinnock's life story. Biden argued that he had simply forgotten to credit Kinnock. He pointed to earlier occasions when he had given the same speech and attributed it properly. But the damage had been done. Journalists found speeches Biden had given that seemed to use the words of political leaders Robert Kennedy and Hubert Humphrey. Some reporters even discovered Biden's failure to cite a source in a law school assignment. The conclusion seemed clear: Biden was a plagiarist.

Biden hoped that the scandal would soon subside. He dismissed the allegations as "a tempest in a teapot"[40] and tried to

American soldiers take an Iraqi civilian into custody. Biden's support for US involvement in Iraq in 2002 generated long-lasting anger among some Democrats.

focus on policy issues. But his support was slipping, and matters only got worse. It came to light that Biden had exaggerated his academic credentials at one point, claiming to have three under-graduate degrees and saying that he had been in the top half of his law school class—neither of which was true. Biden also came under fire for remarks he had made about marching in the civil rights movement. Though Biden was an advocate of civil rights, he had not participated in any significant protests. By this time Biden's integrity was under question, and he was too badly wounded to continue. He withdrew from the presidential race in late September.

Biden's run was over. But his ambitions were not. He returned to the Senate and continued to work for causes he believed in. Still, he was not ready to give up on the idea of becoming presi-dent someday. Almost twenty years after his brief 1988 run, he decided to try again.

CHAPTER FOUR

Mr. Vice President

The early 2000s were difficult years for the Democratic Party. Republican George W. Bush won the presidential election in 2000 and then again in 2004. The Republicans also held a majority in both the House and the Senate for much of Bush's presidency. Biden had considered a run for president in 2004 but had chosen to stay in the Senate. Given the struggles his party was having, though, Biden knew it needed a strong presidential candidate for 2008—and he thought he might well be that person.

Biden's initial task, though, was to convince those closest to him that a run would make sense. His family had grown since he first took office. In 1975, during his first term as senator, Biden had met a Wilmington teacher named Jill Jacobs. Jacobs and Biden married in 1977 and had a daughter, Ashley, four years later. Joe knew that his 1988 campaign had been very difficult for Jill and Ashley, along with Hunter and Beau. At the time, Jill did not entirely share her husband's goal of becoming president. "She had never had any great desire to be in the White House,"[41] Joe admitted. He was hesitant to ask his family for permission to run; he feared they would ask him not to.

In the end, Biden's family brought up the subject of a presidential campaign first. In late December 2004, Jill announced that there would be a family meeting. Joe expected that the purpose of the meeting was to tell him not to run.

"We don't want you to go through this again," he imagined his children saying. But when he arrived at the meeting, Joe was shocked to discover that he had it backward. Instead of imploring him not to make a second run for the presidency, his family members were urging him to make another attempt. "We'll support it," Jill said. "We think you're the best person to pull the country together."[42]

Campaigning

Though the next presidential race would not take place until 2008, Biden announced his plans in 2005. "I know that I'm supposed to tell you that I'm not sure," Biden told reporter Bob Schieffer in a television interview. "But, if, in fact, I think that I have a clear shot at winning the nomination by this November or December, then I'm going to seek the nomination."[43] Biden officially entered the Democratic primary in 2007. Several other candidates joined him, with two in particular standing out. First-term senator Barack Obama of Illinois, who had given a compelling speech at the 2004 Democratic National Convention, was hoping to be the nation's first African American president. And most observers agreed that New York senator Hillary Clinton, wife of former president Bill Clinton, was the front-runner thanks to her extensive experience and political contacts.

Much had changed since Biden's earliest campaigns. Most notably, Biden was no longer youthful. The first time he had run for the presidency he had been in his mid-forties, relatively young for a politician. Now, however, Biden was in his mid-sixties. He tried to make his age an advantage by emphasizing his experience, but that argument did not seem to resonate with voters. In addition, Biden made several verbal mistakes that did not help his cause. In early 2007, when asked about his impression of Obama, Biden replied with what he thought was a positive comment. "You got the first mainstream African-American who is articulate and bright and clean and a nice-looking guy," Biden told the interviewer. "I mean, that's a storybook, man."[44] The remark came across as patronizing at best and racist at worst. Comments like this helped give Biden a reputation as someone who often spoke without thinking.

Biden's struggles were reflected in national polls, which typically showed him far behind his Democratic rivals. Nevertheless, Biden persevered. He showed a thorough knowledge of foreign policy during the Democratic debates and earned praise from some members of the media for the level of detail that marked his poli-

Biden stands with his second wife, Jill, and their daughter, Ashley, in 1988. When he considered a campaign for president in 2008, Biden was surprised that Jill was in favor of his running.

Joe Biden's second wife, Jill Jacobs, was born in New Jersey in 1951 but grew up mostly in Pennsylvania. As a young woman she did some modeling, co-owned a bar with her first husband, and briefly considered a career in fashion design, but before long she decided to focus her career on education. She graduated with a degree in English from the University of Delaware and taught for a while at the secondary level. When she and Joe Biden married in 1977, she was a teacher at a Wilmington high school.

While her husband was still serving in the Senate, Jill continued her own education as well, earning two master's degrees and a doctorate. In addition to teaching high school, Jill has also taught emotionally disabled students and been an instructor at a Delaware community college. She has announced that she plans to continue her teaching career even while serving as First Lady. If she does, it will mark the first time in US history that a sitting First Lady has held a paying job.

cies. As journalist Tom Fitzgerald noted approvingly, Biden spoke in "full paragraphs of context instead of sound bites, making issues seem clear rather than simple."[45] In the end, though, his efforts failed. Despite spending a great deal of time in Iowa, the first state to choose its delegates, Biden won just 1 percent of Iowa's votes. Biden officially dropped out that evening. His campaign was over.

A New Role

Following Biden's withdrawal, some observers suggested that Biden would be well suited for a position in a potential Democratic administration. As a long-term senator with an interest in foreign policy, they pointed out, Biden might make an ideal secretary of state. Biden, however, quickly cut off such speculation. Being secretary of state, he said, held no interest for him. Neither did any role in an administration, including the vice presidency. As Biden explained, "I can absolutely say with certainty I would not be anybody's vice president. Period."[46] Once again, Biden prepared to resume his role in the Senate following an unsuccessful presidential campaign.

After Iowa, the remaining candidates continued to fight for the nomination. Biden watched with interest as minor candidates withdrew, leaving the race to just Clinton and Obama. Officially, Biden did not take sides. But Obama, who had evidently forgiven Biden for his earlier comments, seemed particularly interested in speaking to him. Indeed, Obama and Biden chatted twice a week or so during the primary season. "He'd call not so much to ask for advice as to bounce things off me,"[47] Biden said at the time. When Obama won the nomination, he set out to convince Biden to consider taking a role in his administration. More specifically, Obama asked Biden to consider becoming his vice president.

From Obama's perspective, choosing Biden made sense. Obama was young and unproven; Biden was a known quantity who would lend experience to the ticket. Despite having guaranteed just a few months earlier that he would never serve as vice president, Biden agreed to think about the possibility. He knew, however, that many presidents through history have given their vice presidents very little to do. John Kennedy, for example, frequently excluded his vice president, Lyndon Johnson, from policy decisions. And George Washington's vice president, John Adams, complained that the vice presidency was "the most insignificant office that ever the invention of man contrived or his imagination conceived."[48]

Biden did not want to be ignored as Johnson and Adams had been. He had no great desire to be vice president for its own sake, and he decided that he would only accept the role if Obama would consider him a partner in his administration. "I want a commitment from you that in every important decision you'll make," he told Obama, "I'll get to be in the room."[49] Obama quickly agreed; he had already decided that he wanted a vice president who would challenge him where necessary and be involved in setting policy. In the summer of 2008, Biden was formally announced as Obama's running mate.

Victory
Biden got off to a slow start, however. His main issue was speaking without thinking. On one occasion, Biden declared that Hillary Clinton was better qualified for the vice presidency than he was—

leading people to wonder why, in that case, he had been chosen. On another, he talked about Franklin Roosevelt going on television to reassure Americans when the stock market crashed in 1929, although television did not exist at that point and Roosevelt did not become president until 1933. And on a third, he made a joke about Delaware's growing Indian American community that not only fell flat but seemed vaguely racist. Obama quickly grew frustrated with his running mate. "How many times is Biden gonna say something stupid?"[50] he asked his advisers.

But as the campaign continued, Obama began to appreciate Biden's contributions. Where Obama could come across as formal and cerebral, Biden spoke easily to people of all backgrounds. Obama was also impressed with Biden's energy and work ethic. And Biden helped the campaign in a fall debate against the Republican vice presidential candidate, Alaska governor Sarah Palin. "He kept himself in check," wrote commentator John Dickerson, "and he was commanding."[51] In a poll conducted immediately after the debate, 51 percent of respondents said that Biden was the winner, compared to just 34 percent who said it was Palin.

Biden's father spent many years managing car dealerships, and his interest in cars rubbed off onto his eldest son. As a young man, Biden frequently borrowed good-looking cars from his father's inventory to impress his dates. In an interview with *Car and Driver* magazine, he listed the cars he had owned during the 1960s, not only giving the basic information of each car's make, year, and model but also describing its mileage, performance, and features. His prized possession remains a vintage sports car, which Biden described in the interview as "my 1967 Goodwood-green Corvette, 327, 350-horse, with a rear-axle ratio that really gets up and goes." But in the interview—published while he was serving as vice president—Biden regretfully noted a rule that pertains to all vice presidents, no matter how interested in cars they may be. "The Secret Service won't let me drive it," he explained, referring to the Corvette. "I'm not allowed to drive anything. It's the one thing I hate about this job. I'm serious."

Quoted in Jeff Wilser, *The Book of Joe*. New York: Three Rivers, 2017, p. 129.

As it turned out, the election was not especially close. Obama and Biden won 365 electoral votes; the Republican candidate, Arizona senator John McCain, collected just 173. The Democrats won eight of the ten most populous states and collected 10 million more popular votes than McCain and Palin. At a celebratory election night rally in Chicago, Obama singled out Biden for particular praise, calling him "my partner in this journey" and "a man who campaigned from his heart."[52] After thirty-six years in Congress, Joe Biden was now the vice president of the United States.

Vice President

The new administration had plenty of issues to deal with, and Obama and Biden wasted no time establishing an excellent working relationship. Biden took particular responsibility for several assignments, many involving foreign affairs. Over the years Biden had met numerous world leaders and had developed a strong sense of diplomacy. He also understood foreign policy issues quite well. Consequently, Obama kept Biden busy flying to countries such as Russia, Israel, and Colombia to look after American interests. "There are leaders Obama never really warmed up to," wrote journalist Steve Clemons. "Biden tends these relationships."[53]

Biden also had occasional success working with Republicans in Congress. Senate Majority Leader Mitch McConnell of Kentucky once said that his goal was to make Obama a one-term president, and much of the Republican agenda seemed to be based on obstructing the administration. At one point, though, Biden was able to negotiate with McConnell to raise the federal debt ceiling, an important maneuver to stave off economic meltdown. "I don't always agree with [Biden]," McConnell said at the time, "but I do trust him."[54] On another occasion, Biden not only got Republican senator Arlen Specter of Pennsylvania to support a public health plan called the Affordable Care Act but also convinced him to switch parties.

In addition, Biden helped guide Obama's thinking on a number of important issues. Like most Americans in 2008—and even most Democrats of the time—Obama believed that marriage should be

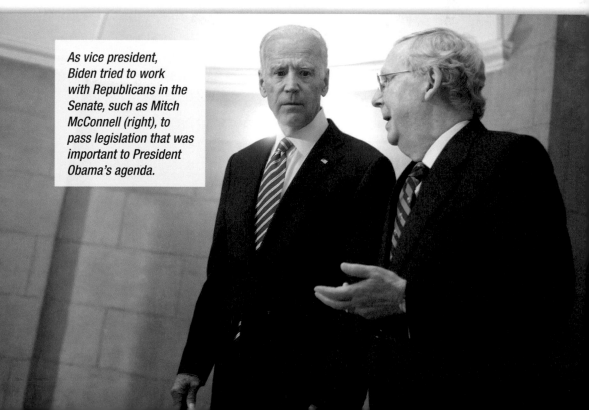

As vice president, Biden tried to work with Republicans in the Senate, such as Mitch McConnell (right), to pass legislation that was important to President Obama's agenda.

reserved for heterosexual couples only. Though he generally favored gay and lesbian rights, he rejected the notion of same-sex marriage. In 2012, however, Biden forced the issue. "Men marrying men, women marrying women, and heterosexual men and women marrying another are entitled to the same exact rights, all the civil rights, all the civil liberties,"[55] Biden said in an interview. Following his vice president's lead, Obama soon came to support marriage equality. By 2020, according to polling conducted by the Gallup organization, 67 percent of Americans supported same-sex marriage.

Reelection and Tragedy

Obama and Biden won a second term in 2012 against former Massachusetts governor Mitt Romney and one-time Speaker of the House Paul Ryan. As the 2016 election approached, political leaders began to speculate about Biden's next move. Though Biden had already lost two runs for the presidential nomination, commentators suspected that he might make another try once Obama was out of office. By now Biden was both well known and popular, and the economy was doing well. Historically speaking, moreover, when two-term presidents leave office, their vice presidents frequently run to succeed them. Vice President George H.W. Bush, for instance, ran in 1988 to replace Reagan, and Al Gore ran in 2000 after serving two terms under Bill Clinton.

But as the 2016 election approached, Biden had a more important issue on his mind. In 2013 his son Beau Biden had been diagnosed with brain cancer. Despite radiation and chemotherapy treatments, the cancer grew, and Beau died in May 2015. That fall, Joe Biden announced that he would not seek the presidential nomination. Anyone running for president, Biden explained, needed to be able to say to the American people, "I promise you have my whole heart, my whole soul, my energy, and my passion."[56] Given his grief, Biden believed that he could not in good conscience offer those things to voters. In January 2017 his term as vice president came to an end. He was out of public service for the first time since 1970. At the time, it seemed to mark the final step in an illustrious political career.

CHAPTER FIVE

President Biden

After leaving the vice presidency, Biden joined the faculty of the University of Pennsylvania. He also wrote a book and spearheaded efforts to find effective treatments for cancer. He remained active in politics as well, offering support to Democrats seeking election to Congress and speaking out on important issues. His political commentary was particularly pointed because the 2016 presidential election was won by Republican businessman Donald Trump. Biden saw Trump as a bully who despised women, immigrants, and people of color and represented a serious threat to the country's stability, unity, and values. "We're walking down a very dark path,"[57] Biden warned in a speech given during Trump's first year as president.

Given Biden's high profile and strident criticism of Trump, some observers began asking him if he might try yet again to run for president in 2020. At first Biden was noncommittal. He worried, once again, about the effect a campaign might have on his family. On the other hand, Biden believed that his experience and reputation made him well suited to take on Trump. In the end the desire to run won out, and in April 2019 Biden officially launched his campaign. "We are in a battle for the soul of this nation,"[58] he declared in a video announcing his intentions.

The Primary Season

The Democratic primary field was unusually crowded, but as the best-known candidate, Biden led the early polls. When the Democrats started to debate during the summer of 2019, how-ever, his support began to drop. Viewers of the earliest debates saw Biden as passive and somewhat inarticulate. It did not help that other candidates frequently singled him out for attack. For ex-ample, at one point California senator Kamala Harris reminded the audience of Biden's long-standing opposition to mandatory school busing, saying, "There was a little girl in California who was part of the second class to integrate her public schools, and she was bused to school every day. And that little girl was me."[59]

Matters soon grew worse. In February 2020 Biden finished a distant fourth in Iowa, the first contest of the primary season. The following week Biden came in fifth in New Hampshire. And though Biden finished second later that month in Nevada, he got just 18 percent of the vote. Luckily for Biden, the final contest of February was scheduled for South Carolina, a state where African Americans made up the majority of Democratic primary voters. Because of his long-standing support for civil rights and his con-nection to Obama, Biden had always been popular among Black voters. Biden pointed out that Iowa, Nevada, and New Hampshire had few Black residents and argued that the next contest would show that he was still a contender. "I will win South Carolina,"[60] he stated in a debate shortly before the primary.

> "There was a little girl in California who was part of the second class to integrate her public schools, and she was bused to school every day."[59]
>
> —Kamala Harris, senator from California

He was right. Backed by enthusiastic support from African Americans, Biden won a convincing victory in South Carolina. Next he won ten of the fifteen contests held on March 3. Recognizing Biden's strength, several of his rivals dropped out of the race dur-ing this period; three of them endorsed Biden for the nomination. The only serious candidate left was Vermont senator Bernie Sand-ers, but when Biden won eight of the next ten primaries, Sanders withdrew as well. Fifty years after his first political campaign, Biden was on his way to becoming the Democratic presidential nominee.

Biden appears onstage in 2019 with nine other candidates vying for the Democratic nomination for president.

Biden's next task was to choose a running mate. Earlier in the race he had promised to pick a woman, and in August he decided on Kamala Harris, the senator who had challenged him on busing the previous summer. In introducing her, Biden praised Harris as a "fearless fighter for the little guy, and one of the country's finest public servants."[61] Harris also brought several particular strengths to the ticket. One was her relative youth; born in 1964, Harris was a generation younger than Biden. Another was her background as a prosecutor, which Biden believed would appeal to political moderates. And third was Harris's ethnic background. As the child of an Indian mother and a Jamaican father, Harris was attractive to Black and Asian American voters.

Campaigning in a Pandemic

The 2020 presidential campaign was like no other in American history. The main reason was the COVID-19 pandemic that had begun sweeping the nation earlier that year. COVID-19 was both infectious and dangerous, and in early 2020 there was no vaccine and no reliable treatment. Medical experts advised people to stay inside and to wear masks if they had to go out. Many states and

Early in the 2020 campaign, several women alleged that Biden had touched them inappropriately and in ways that made them feel uncomfortable. Nevada politician Lucy Flores, for example, charged that Biden had put his hands on her shoulders and kissed the back of her head without her consent. Other women had similar stories—Biden had given them unwanted hugs, run his hand along their backs, or touched their bodies in other ways that felt overly intimate. And one former Biden staff member, Tara Reade, said that she had been sexually assaulted by Biden in 1993.

Biden strongly denied Reade's allegations, and a number of media outlets that investigated her assertions—including Vox, the *Nation*, and Politico—cast significant doubt on Reade's truthfulness. Biden took the other charges more seriously, however. He willingly acknowledged that he was often quite physical with other people, including those he did not know well, and admitted that he might have made some people uncomfortable. "We have arrived at an important time when women can and should relate their experiences," Biden said, referring to the growing #MeToo movement that focused on sexual harassment and assault, "and men should pay attention. And I will."

Quoted in Neil Vigdor, "Connecticut Woman Says Then-Vice President Joe Biden Touched Her Inappropriately at a Greenwich Fundraiser in 2009," *Hartford (CT) Courant*, April 1, 2019. www.courant.com.

cities closed schools and businesses. Sports leagues played in empty stadiums; for millions, social distancing became a way of life. Still, the disease spread rapidly. By the end of January 2021 almost 26 million Americans had been infected, and more than 435,000 were dead.

The COVID-19 pandemic deeply affected the race between Biden and Trump. Normally, political candidates spend their time campaigning in person. They meet individually with voters or donors, hold rallies for enthusiastic supporters, and speak to thousands at political conventions. The medical world, however, urged candidates to avoid these activities in 2020. Biden accordingly remained home, giving speeches and interviews via the internet. The Democrats replaced their regular convention with televised videos. "The American people look to [Biden] to set an example," said a Democratic official, "and if the public health advice is that everybody ought to wear a mask, Joe

Biden recognizes the strength of his reach and the degree to which people look to him to lead."[62]

Trump, on the other hand, rejected the consensus of the medical establishment. He worried about how the economic effects of closing businesses would affect his campaign, and he downplayed the seriousness of COVID-19. "It's going to disappear," he assured the nation in February 2020. "One day—it's like a miracle—it will disappear."[63] Trump refused to wear a mask and held large rallies beginning in June. Against medical advice, the Republicans even tried unsuccessfully to hold an in-person convention. The contrast between the two campaigns was impossible to miss.

The pandemic had a more direct political impact as well. Most states made it much easier for people to vote early or by mail, thus avoiding potential COVID-19 transmission on Election Day. Biden strongly encouraged voters to take advantage of these opportunities. Trump, however, advised his supporters to vote in

In August 2020, Biden announced his choice of Kamala Harris as his running mate, fulfilling his promise to pick a woman to run as vice president.

person on Election Day. Trump also charged that allowing early and mail-in ballots would open the door to voter fraud, although he had difficulty articulating how. These competing messages meant that most Republicans planned to vote on Election Day, while most Democrats did not—a split that would have consequences down the road.

Other Issues

Biden's position on how to respond to the pandemic differed sharply from Trump's, but in truth the candidates disagreed on virtually every issue. Biden, for example, supported the Affordable Care Act, while Trump tried to eliminate it. Biden encouraged immigration; Trump wanted to build a wall along the entire US-Mexico border. Biden was sympathetic to the concerns of the Black Lives Matter movement, whereas Trump dismissed the protesters as thugs. From foreign policy to the environment and from energy issues to tax cuts, the two men diverged—often wildly—on the direction America should take.

But policy disagreements were overshadowed by the relentlessly negative—and often personal—tone of the 2020 campaign. In 2016 Trump had routinely used offensive language to disparage his opponents. Trump tried the same strategy with Biden, calling him "Sleepy Joe" and "Basement Biden."[64] He frequently asserted that Biden had dementia and said that Biden should be imprisoned for unspecified crimes. Biden responded with anger on several occasions, most notably during a debate in the early fall. "Will you shut up, man?" he snapped at one point when Trump interrupted him. Biden also characterized Trump as a "clown" and "the worst president America has ever had."[65]

The campaign was also notable for Trump's repeated statements that he might not abide by the election results if he lost. He alleged again and again that the Democrats were engaging in voter fraud. Trump also refused to promise a peaceful transition of power should Biden be the winner. Several times he argued, in direct violation of the Constitution, that he should have three terms as president. "We

The Electoral College

The United States selects its presidents based on a system known as the Electoral College. In this system each state is given a certain number of electoral votes based on its representation in Congress—which in turn is based on its population. A state gets one electoral vote for each of its two Senate seats and one for each of its seats in the House of Representatives. Small states like Delaware, for instance, have two senators and one representative and are entitled to three electoral votes. At the other end of the scale, California, which has two senators and fifty-three representatives, had fifty-five electoral votes in 2020.

Except in Nebraska and Maine, all electoral votes in a state are awarded to the candidate who wins the most votes statewide. Whichever candidate receives the greatest number of electoral votes is the overall winner. It is quite possible for a candidate to win the popular vote nationwide and lose in the Electoral College if he or she wins some large states by a lot and narrowly loses others. Most recently, Democrats Hillary Clinton in 2016 and Al Gore in 2000 won the popular vote but lost the election.

are going to win four more years," he promised in August. "And then after that, we'll go for another four years because they spied on my campaign."[66] Trump's rhetoric in this regard alarmed Biden and his supporters, since it undermined the very idea of democracy.

Election Night and Beyond

Election night came and went without a winner. Millions of votes were cast early, but in some states, such as Pennsylvania, the Election Day ballots were counted first. These were largely for Trump, as anticipated, and Trump quickly opened up what seemed to be a big lead in these states. On this basis, he declared victory. News anchors and election experts quickly pushed back against this claim, however, pointing out that ballots not yet counted would likely favor Biden. As more votes were tallied, they noted, Trump's lead would dwindle or disappear altogether. Biden remained optimistic. "We believe we're on track to win this election," Biden said. "It ain't over 'til every vote is counted."[67]

Before long, Biden took slender leads in Pennsylvania and other key states. Within a few days it became clear that Biden had won the election. Not only did he receive about 7 million more votes than Trump—Biden's total of 81 million votes was the most in American history—but more importantly, he defeated Trump 306–232 in the Electoral College. Biden declared victory. "I will be a President for all Americans—whether you voted for me or not," he promised via Twitter. "I will keep the faith that you have placed in me."[68] Just as he had threatened, however, Trump proved unwilling to accept the results. On December 12, for example, he proclaimed in a tweet, "I WON THE ELECTION IN A LANDSLIDE."[69]

Trump tried to overturn the election. His supporters alleged that undocumented aliens had cast millions of ballots, that voting machines had been set to change Trump votes into Biden votes, that the Biden campaign had stuffed the ballot boxes for Biden, and much more. Trump and his allies filed dozens of lawsuits asking that the election results be thrown out, but they lost almost every case. Recounts in several states failed to change Biden's victory. Trump unsuccessfully urged Georgia election officials to award him nearly twelve thousand votes that had not actually been cast. Trump and his supporters grew more and more angry. On January 6, 2021, with Congress about to certify the election results, protesters stormed the Capitol in an effort to reverse Biden's victory. Many were armed and prepared for violence. Chaos ensued, and several people died before order was restored.

> "I will be a President for all Americans—whether you voted for me or not. I will keep the faith that you have placed in me."[68]
>
> —Joe Biden

A New President

Through it all Biden remained focused on his upcoming presidency. He outlined his priorities, such as controlling COVID-19, overturning Trump-era restrictions on immigration, and working for racial justice. He also began revealing his picks for his

With his hand on the Bible held by his wife, Joe Biden takes the oath of office of President of the United States on January 20, 2021.

cabinet—the people who would serve as his closest advisers. It was a remarkably diverse group. Of the fifteen nominees, only four were non-Hispanic White men—and of these, two were Jewish and one was openly gay. Many nominees had served in the Obama administration, and Biden knew most of them personally. The nominees also had plenty of experience in government. "Biden's picks are capable, sensible and play well in the sandbox together,"[70] says a former Obama adviser.

On January 20, 2021, Biden took his oath of office. Due to the pandemic and threats of violence, the inauguration was sparsely attended—but millions followed the event electronically. In his speech Biden emphasized unity, respect, and responsibility, along with the need to preserve American democracy and a clear reckoning of the job that lay ahead. "With purpose and resolve we turn to the tasks of our time," he said in closing. "Sustained by faith. Driven by conviction. And, devoted to each other and to this country we love with all our hearts."[71]

For Biden, the inauguration was the culmination of a lifetime in public service that had begun with a run for county commissioner fifty years before. He had faced disappointment and tragedy, yet he had never given up. At an age when most people are retired, Biden had the energy and the drive to take on the challenges of being America's forty-sixth president. Becoming president was a remarkable achievement—but only one of many in a remarkable life.

SOURCE NOTES

Introduction: The President and the Man

1. Quoted in Aram Roston and Mark Makela, "Thousands Take to Streets of U.S. in Celebration of Biden Victory," *U.S. News & World Report*, November 7, 2020. www.usnews.com.
2. Zachary B. Wolf, "America Is Going from an Outsider President to the Ultimate Insider," CNN, December 5, 2020. www.cnn.com.
3. Quoted in Nancy Benac, "Biden's Prism of Loss: A Public Man, Shaped by Private Grief," AP News, August 18, 2019. https://apnews.com.
4. Quoted in *New York Times*, "Joseph R. Biden Jr.'s Convention Speech," August 27, 2008. www.nytimes.com.

Chapter One: Early Years

5. Joe Biden, *Promises to Keep*. New York: Random House, 2007, p. 11.
6. Biden, *Promises to Keep*, p. xxii.
7. Quoted in Jeff Wilser, *The Book of Joe*. New York: Three Rivers, 2017, p. 4.
8. Biden, *Promises to Keep*, p. 8.
9. Biden, *Promises to Keep*, p. 3.
10. Biden, *Promises to Keep*, p. 20.
11. Quoted in Lochlahn Marsh, "A Look Back at Joe Biden's Days as an Athlete," *Daily Pennsylvanian* (University of Pennsylvania), August 20, 2020. www.thedp.com.
12. Quoted in John M. Broder, "Father's Tough Life an Inspiration for Biden," *New York Times*, October 24, 2008. www.nytimes.com.
13. Quoted in Wilser, *The Book of Joe*, p. 18.
14. Quoted in Howard Kurtz, "Sen. Biden May Try to Talk His Way into the White House," *Washington Post*, July 28, 1986. www.washingtonpost.com.
15. Quoted in Charles Moritz, ed., *Current Biography Yearbook 1987*. New York: Wilson, 1988, p. 43.

Chapter Two: Politics and Tragedy

16. Quoted in Kate Sheehy, "How Biden Went from Small-Time Councilman to the White House," *New York Post*, November 7, 2020. https://nypost.com.
17. Biden, *Promises to Keep*, p. 50.
18. Biden, *Promises to Keep*, p. 51.
19. Biden, *Promises to Keep*, p. 58.
20. William B. Golin, "How Joe Biden Changed Delaware's—and America's—Politics," Delaware Online, November 27, 2020. www.delawareonline.com.
21. Quoted in Brian Naylor, "Biden's Road to Senate Took Tragic Turn," NPR, October 8, 2007. www.npr.org.
22. Quoted in Moritz, *Current Biography Yearbook 1987*, p. 43.
23. Quoted in Wilser, *The Book of Joe*, pp. 36–37.
24. Quoted in Golin, "How Joe Biden Changed Delaware's—and America's—Politics."
25. Biden, *Promises to Keep*, p. 78.
26. Biden, *Promises to Keep*, p. 80.
27. Quoted in Wilser, *The Book of Joe*, p. 49.

Chapter Three: Senator Biden

28. Biden, *Promises to Keep*, pp. 87–88.
29. Quoted in Wilser, *The Book of Joe*, p. 61.
30. Quoted in Todd S. Purdum, "The Old Senate Is Hard-Wired into Joe Biden," *The Atlantic*, June 21, 2019. www.theatlantic.com.
31. Quoted in Sara Fritz, "Shultz, Senators Clash over South Africa," *Los Angeles Times*, July 24, 1986. www.latimes.com.
32. Quoted in Tara Law, "The Violence Against Women Act Was Signed 25 Years Ago. Here's How the Law Changed American Culture," *Time*, September 12, 2019. https://time.com.
33. Quoted in Moritz, *Current Biography Yearbook 1987*, p. 44.
34. Biden, *Promises to Keep*, p. 111.
35. Quoted in Paul Taylor, "Biden a 'Regular Guy' with Regular-Guy Flaws," *Washington Post*, September 20, 1987. www.washingtonpost.com.
36. Quoted in Kate Phillips, "Biden and Anita Hill, Revisited," *New York Times*, August 23, 2008. www.nytimes.com.
37. Mark Weisbrot, "Joe Biden Championed the Iraq War. Will That Come Back to Haunt Him Now?," *The Guardian* (Manchester, UK), February 17, 2020. www.theguardian.com.
38. Quoted in E.J. Dionne, "Biden Joins Campaign for the Presidency," *New York Times*, June 10, 1987. www.nytimes.com.
39. Quoted in Matthew Yglesias, "The Joe Biden Climate Change Plagiarism 'Scandal,' Explained," Vox, June 5, 2019. www.vox.com.

40. Quoted in David Greenberg, "Why Biden's Plagiarism Shouldn't Be Forgotten," *Slate*, August 25, 2008. https://slate.com.

Chapter Four: Mr. Vice President
41. Biden, *Promises to Keep*, p. 180.
42. Quoted in Biden, *Promises to Keep*, pp. 358–59.
43. Quoted in Ron Elving, "Biden: His Time?," NPR, June 21, 2005. www.npr.org.
44. Quoted in *Time*, "Top 10 Joe Biden Gaffes," January 31, 2007. http://content.time.com.
45. Quoted in Wilser, *The Book of Joe*, p. 124.
46. Quoted in Mark Bowden, "The Salesman," *The Atlantic*, October 2010. www.theatlantic.com.
47. Quoted in Ryan Lizza, "Biden's Brief," *New Yorker*, October 20, 2008. www.newyorker.com.
48. Quoted in Jaime Fuller, "Here Are a Bunch of Awful Things Vice Presidents Have Said About Being No. 2," *Washington Post*, October 3, 2014. www.washingtonpost.com.
49. Quoted in Wilser, *The Book of Joe*, p. 128.
50. Quoted in Wilser, *The Book of Joe*, p. 135.
51. John Dickerson, "Champ vs. Doggone," *Slate*, October 3, 2008. https://slate.com.
52. Quoted in NPR, "Transcript of Barack Obama's Victory Speech," November 5, 2008. www.npr.org.
53. Quoted in Wilser, *The Book of Joe*, p. 145.
54. Quoted in Wilser, *The Book of Joe*, p. 150.
55. Quoted in CBS News, "Politicians Who've Flip-Flopped on Same-Sex Marriages," 2021. www.cbsnews.com.
56. Quoted in Wilser, *The Book of Joe*, p. 165.

Chapter Five: President Biden
57. Quoted in David Smith, "'We're Walking Down a Dark Path': Biden Hammers Trump in Scathing Speech," *The Guardian* (Manchester, UK), October 5, 2017. www.theguardian.com.
58. Quoted in Michael Scherer and John Wagner, "Former Vice President Joe Biden Jumps into White House Race," *Washington Post*, April 25, 2019. www.washingtonpost.com.
59. Quoted in Salvador Rizzo, "The School Busing Debate Between Joe Biden and Kamala Harris," *Washington Post*, July 29, 2019. www.washingtonpost.com.
60. Quoted in Sean Collins, "Who Is Going to Win the South Carolina Primary, According to the Polls," *Vox*, February 29, 2020. www.vox.com.

61. Quoted in Alexandra Jaffe and Will Weissert, "Joe Biden and Kamala Harris: Ex-VP and California Senator Are the Democrats Who Will Take on Trump and Pence," *Chicago Tribune*, August 11, 2020. www.chicagotribune.com.
62. Quoted in MaryAlice Parks, "The Striking Difference Between the Democratic and Republican Conventions," ABC News, August 27, 2020. https://abcnews.go.com.
63. Quoted in Daniel Wolfe and Daniel Dale, "'It's Going to Disappear': A Timeline of Trump's Claims That COVID-19 Will Vanish," CNN, October 31, 2020. www.cnn.com.
64. Quoted in Joseph Curl, "Joe Biden's Basement Strategy Really Is His Plan," *Washington Times,* October 27, 2020. www.washingtontimes.com.
65. Quoted in Lara Seligman et al., "The Most Bitter Clashes from Trump and Biden's First Debate Showdown," Politico, September 29, 2020. www.politico.com.
66. Quoted in Kevin Liptak, "A List of the Times Trump Has Said He Won't Accept the Election Results or Leave Office If He Loses," CNN, September 24, 2020. www.cnn.com.
67. Quoted in Tamara Keith et al., "Race Up in the Air, Even as Trump Falsely Claims Victory," NPR, November 4, 2020. www.npr.org.
68. Quoted in Jonathan Lemire and Zeke Miller, "AP: Joe Biden Declared Winner of 2020 Presidential Election," Boston 25 News, November 7, 2020. www.boston25news.com.
69. Quoted in Joe Price, "Trump Still Tweeting Claims About the Election Being 'Stolen,' Takes Aim at GOP Governors," Complex, December 12, 2020. www.complex.com.
70. Quoted in Jonathan Lemire, "Analysis: Biden Prioritizes Experience with Cabinet Picks," AP News, November 25, 2020. https://apnews.com.
71. Joe Biden, "Inaugural Address by President Joseph R. Biden, Jr.," White House, January 20, 2020. www.whitehouse.gov.

IMPORTANT EVENTS IN THE LIFE OF JOE BIDEN

1942
Joseph Robinette Biden Jr. is born on November 20 in Pennsylvania.

1953
The Biden family moves to Delaware.

1961
Biden graduates from Archmere Academy and begins attending the University of Delaware.

1966
Joe Biden and Neilia Hunter marry.

1968
Biden graduates from Syracuse University College of Law.

1972
Biden's wife, Neilia, and their daughter, Naomi, are killed in a car accident; their two sons, Beau and Hunter, are badly injured but survive.

1973
Biden is sworn in as a US senator from Delaware.

1977
Joe Biden and Jill Jacobs marry.

1979
Biden helps negotiate an arms control treaty with the Soviet Union.

1987
Biden enters and then drops out of his first presidential race.

1988
Biden undergoes emergency brain surgery at Walter Reed Army Medical Center for an aneurysm.

1991
As chair of the Senate Judiciary Committee, Biden leads tumultuous confirmation hearings for Supreme Court associate justice Clarence Thomas, who was accused of sexual harassment.

1994
The Violence Against Women Act, originally sponsored by Biden, passes both houses of Congress. The act is a package of laws against domestic violence.

2002
Biden joins most members of Congress in authorizing a declaration of war against Iraq.

2007
Biden's memoir *Promises to Keep: On Life and Politics* is published; Biden enters his second presidential race but later drops out.

2008
Barack Obama and Joe Biden are elected president and vice president.

2012
Obama and Biden are reelected president and vice president.

2015
Biden's eldest son, Beau Biden, dies from brain cancer at age forty-six; Biden announces he will not seek the presidential nomination for the 2016 election.

2019
Biden enters the race for the Democratic nomination for president.

2020
Biden defeats Donald Trump in the race for president.

2021
Biden is sworn in as president, and Kamala Harris is sworn in as vice president.

FOR FURTHER RESEARCH

Books

Joe Biden, *Promise Me, Dad: A Year of Hope, Hardship, and Purpose*. New York: Flatiron, 2018.

Joe Biden, *Promises to Keep: On Life and Politics*. New York: Random House, 2008.

Ryan Gale, *Joe Biden: 46th US President*. Minneapolis, MN: ABDO, 2021.

Evan Osnos, *Joe Biden: The Life, the Run, and What Matters Now*. New York: Scribner, 2020.

Internet Sources

Brian Contreras, "From the Coronavirus to the Environment, Biden Plans to Take Government in New Direction," *Los Angeles Times*, November 24, 2020. www.latimes.com.

Marc Fisher, "The Two Sides of Joe Biden," *Washington Post*, January 13, 2021. www.washingtonpost.com.

Katie Glueck and Thomas Kaplan, "A President-Elect Shaped by Tragedy and Tradition," *New York Times*, November 14, 2020. www.nytimes.com.

John Hendrickson, "What Joe Biden Can't Bring Himself to Say," *The Atlantic*, January–February 2020. www.theatlantic.com.

Washington Post Staff, "Joe Biden and Kamala Harris: A Rundown of Their Family, Policy Stances and History in Office," *Washington Post*, January 21, 2021. www.washingtonpost.com.

Websites

Ballotpedia (https://ballotpedia.org/Joe_Biden). This website includes information and links to articles about Joe Biden's personal and professional life, including past elections and legislative actions throughout his career.

Frontline (www.pbs.org/wgbh/frontline/film/president-biden). This PBS television program offers access to dozens of its interviews, documentaries, and news reports about Joe Biden, his policies, his personal history, and his election and inauguration as president.

History Channel (www.history.com/topics/us-presidents). This website features information about American presidents and presidential elections throughout US history.

Presidential Libraries (www.archives.gov/presidential-libraries/research /alic/presidents.html). This website of the National Archives features links to information about presidential documents, US presidents, and presidential libraries. The site also has links to information about First Ladies and the salaries and retirement benefits of US presidents.

INDEX

PICTURE CREDITS